T0197411

Thought Power

A Child's Guide to Thought Control for Victorious Christian Living

Peggy Callender Clyne

Copyright © 2015 Margaret Clyne.

All rights reserved. No part of this book may be used or reproduced by any means, graphic, electronic, or mechanical, including photocopying, recording, taping or by any information storage retrieval system without the written permission of the author except in the case of brief quotations embodied in critical articles and reviews.

Scripture taken from the King James Version of the Bible.

Scripture taken from the Holy Bible, NEW INTERNATIONAL VERSION®. Copyright © 1973, 1978, 1984 by Biblica, Inc. All rights reserved worldwide. Used by permission. NEW INTERNATIONAL VERSION® and NIV® are registered trademarks of Biblica, Inc. Use of either trademark for the offering of goods or services requires the prior written consent of Biblica US, Inc.

Scripture taken from the Contemporary English Version © 1991, 1992, 1995 by American Bible Society, Used by Permission.

WestBow Press books may be ordered through booksellers or by contacting:

WestBow Press
A Division of Thomas Nelson & Zondervan
1663 Liberty Drive
Bloomington, IN 47403
www.westbowpress.com
1 (866) 928-1240

Because of the dynamic nature of the Internet, any web addresses or links contained in this book may have changed since publication and may no longer be valid. The views expressed in this work are solely those of the author and do not necessarily reflect the views of the publisher, and the publisher hereby disclaims any responsibility for them.

Any people depicted in stock imagery provided by Thinkstock are models, and such images are being used for illustrative purposes only. Certain stock imagery © Thinkstock.

ISBN: 978-1-5127-1341-1 (sc)
ISBN: 978-1-5127-1342-8 (e)
Library of Congress Control Number: 2015915686

Print information available on the last page.

WestBow Press rev. date: 10/26/2015

DEDICATION

To ALL THE CHILDREN in my life, and to children EVERYWHERE who have accepted or will accept Jesus Christ as their personal Saviour and Lord. This book is written to help you program your mind for victorious Christian living.

To the children's PARENTS, I pray that you will reinforce the

Thought Power philosophy in word and in deed.

Finally, to SENIOR CITIZENS, go for it! You are NOT too old! Write that book! Paint that landscape! Start that business! Declare with Caleb, "Give me this mountain!" (Joshua 14:12)

Table of Contents

FOREWORD

In a world where our moral and spiritual values are being undermined by the absence of good parenting, the World Wide Web, and immoral television shows, our children are left to grow up with a void of those essential values that make them better at living life. *Thought Power* helps fill that void.

Although we are NOT our thoughts, our thoughts do have POWER! Peggy seeks to prepare children to live lives that are guided by Biblical principles and Christian values. Through *Thought Power*, children will learn how to think clean and Godly thoughts. And as we all know, we act and speak as we think.

Whether this book is used by parents in the home, teachers in schools, or ministers in church, *Thought Power* will add value to the learning experience of children everywhere.

It is my prayer that every parent, teacher, minister who reads this book to our children, and every child who reads this book on their own, will use their thought power to improve their lives and advance the Kingdom of God.

Bishop John I. Cline

Senior Pastor, New Life Baptist Church

Tortola, British Virgin Islands

ACKNOWLEDGEMENTS

I thank ---

God for this idea and the ability to execute it;

My husband, Freddie, our children -- all the family – for their cooperation; grandchildren Kailah, Akeel, Isaiah, ThaiKristina, and Jaide (the "Baby Grand"), friends Julia and Levi Maree and Pastor and Mrs. Gerhardus Maree for their cooperation;

My cousin and pastor, Bishop John I. Cline for writing the Foreword;

The ladies in the Prevailing Empowerment Circle Network (PECN) for seeding into this project;

Brenda Cline for her extraordinary illustrations; and Hezikiah Maddox and Dawn Simmon-Michael for their photographic genius.

Last, but not least, I thank Karen Bell, Paul Backshall and the staff at Caribbean Printing Company (BVI) for printing the original edition of *Thought Power* in 2002 making all subsequent versions believable!

God bless you all!

INTRODUCTION

The objective of this book is to teach youngsters the relationship between thought control and victorious Christian living. There is much in the market today about positive thinking and visualization. This book attempts to give children an early start at learning to control their thoughts, which will determine their attitude towards the things of God, as well as towards people in general. In addition, it teaches children that they have purpose; that God has a plan for their lives even as children. They can learn now to think and speak Biblically and to visualize and act out that which is positive and Christ-like. I believe this book will help the reader live a more victorious Christian life.

Even children experience a kind of "spiritual warfare" – that tug of choosing between "right" and "wrong." As a result, the inspiration verse I've chosen for this book is Ephesians 4:23 (NIV): "And be made new in the attitude of your mind." When children realize that their thoughts are powerful and literally direct the course of their lives, I think they will be inspired to use their "Thought Power" to its highest potential.

WHO AM I?

On a far-away island in the Caribbean, a man and his wife live in a pale blue house near the beach. His name is "Pop-Pop". Her name is "Granny".

Pop-Pop likes to strum on his guitars. Granny likes to bake bread.

My name is Kailah. Can you guess what I like to do? I like to ask questions!

One day I asked, "Pop-Pop, who am I?"

"You are my special granddaughter", Pop-Pop answered.

"If I am so special, Pop-Pop, why did Pastor say I'm a sinner?"

"Well, Kailah", Pop-Pop explained, "we were born with a sinful nature. We like to have our own way. We don't want anyone telling us what to do -- not even God! Sometimes we lie, we cheat, we hurt other people. But God loved us so much that He sent His Son Jesus Christ to die on the cross for our sin. Then Jesus arose from the dead with ALL POWER! When we ask Him to forgive our sin, He does. It's called being **'born again'**. We become a child of God and He gives us power. Power to obey Him. Power to tell the truth. Power to play fair. Power to help people instead of hurting people. He gives us power to make right choices. I call it THOUGHT POWER."

WHY AM I HERE?

"Granny, why did God make me?"

Granny said: "God made you because He wanted someone to love Him. He wanted someone like Himself in His world. Someone to make a difference in someone else's life. He has a wonderful plan for your life, Kailah. When you ask Jesus to be your Saviour, it's because He chose you. The Bible says, we love Him because He first loved us." (First John 4:19.)

"Jesus wants to be your **Best Friend**. Can you imagine introducing your Friend Jesus to other people? Memorize John 3:16 in your Bible. (For God so loved the world, that he gave his only begotten son; that whosoever believeth in him, should not perish but have everlasting life.) Think about sharing God's love. Remember: You have THOUGHT POWER!"

WHY ARE MY THOUGHTS IMPORTANT?

I still had a LOT of questions about "Thought Power". So I asked Granny why are thoughts so important? Granny said she and Pop-Pop used to hear their Pastor say:

Watch your thoughts because they become words;

Watch your words because they become actions;

Watch your actions because they become habits;

Watch your habits because they become character;

Watch your character because it becomes your destiny.

Something I do all the time is called a "habit". "Character" means the kind of person I am. It's my personality. "Destiny" means my future.

Where am I going? I am going wherever my thoughts take me. My thoughts are my leaders. It's like the game, "Follow the Leader". Granny says my thoughts are just like that. They lead me and I follow.

I will obey.

I will tell the truth.

I will be kind.

When I think honest thoughts, it's easy to tell the truth. But whenever I think about lying, I tell lies. When I think happy thoughts, I get along with my friends. But whenever I think angry, mean thoughts, I end up fussing or fighting. I'm going to be careful what I think about. I'll ask God to help me. After all, He's the one who gave me THOUGHT POWER!

HOW CAN I TEST MY THOUGHTS?

Thoughts are in my head all day! I know that some are good thoughts and some are not so good. Pop-Pop said I can test my thoughts by asking myself questions:

1. What does the Bible say about my thought?
2. What would probably happen if I prayed my thought to God? Would He be happy or sad?
3. Have I learned anything in Sunday School or Children's Church about my thought?
4. Suppose people could SEE my thought? Suppose they could see right into my head! Would I like them to know what I am thinking?

HOW DO I LEARN MY PURPOSE?

Granny said one way to learn my purpose is by **reading the Bible**. It's a book about God and how He gets along with people. Granny calls it having a **"relationship"**. Can you picture yourself having a relationship with God? I can! Oh, yes, I can!

Along with Bible reading, I must **pray**. Prayer is talking and listening to God. I can do that any time and any place. I can tell God everything because He's my Best Friend. I will pray to God and say: "God, please teach me your purpose. And help me use THOUGHT POWER to obey you."

Another way to know God's purpose is to **go to church**. When I go to Children's Church, I hear a Bible story. My teacher tells me what the story means. I think about what she says. I try to SEE it in my mind. When I SEE it in my mind it helps me to DO it.

Pop-Pop said **helping others** is another way to learn my purpose. Who do I like to help? What do I like to do? The Bible says "Even a child is known by his doings…" (Proverbs 20:11).

Sometimes **talking to other people** helps me know God's purpose. God may speak to me through a friend. Some friends are "good company". Some are not. I can choose good friends because I have THOUGHT POWER. Granny said:

◊ Good friends are kind.
◊ Good friends are honest.
◊ Good friends respect you, and they want good things to happen to you.
◊ Good friends usually have good manners.

That's what Granny said.

I thank God for THOUGHT POWER. I can know
His plan for my life. I can be a **winner!**

DAILY POWER PRAYER

Dear Lord,

Thank you for Thought Power.
I can THINK what is right,
I can SPEAK what is pure,
I can DO what is excellent, praiseworthy, and more.

Help me THINK what is right,
Help me SPEAK what is pure,
Help me DO what is excellent, and win battles galore.
In Jesus' Name.

Amen.

BIBLE VERSES

WHO AM I? – Psalm 139:14 (NIV) I praise you because I am fearfully and wonderfully made; your works are wonderful, I know that full well.

WHY AM I HERE? Ephesians 2:10 (NIV) For we are God's workmanship, created in Christ Jesus to do good works, which God prepared in advance for us to do.

WHY ARE MY THOUGHTS IMPORTANT? – Proverbs 23:7a (KJV) For as he thinketh in his heart, so is he.

HOW CAN I TEST MY THOUGHTS? – Philippians 4:8 (NIV) Finally, brothers, whatever is true, whatever is noble, whatever is right, whatever is pure, whatever is lovely, whatever is admirable—if anything is excellent or praiseworthy—think about such things.

HOW DO I LEARN MY PURPOSE? Romans 12:2 (Contemporary English Version) Don't be like the people of this world, but let God change the way you think. Then you will know how to do everything that is good and pleasing to him.

CONTACT INFORMATION

Peggy Clyne
P.O. Box 11156 – PMB 129
c/o Rush-It, Inc.
St. Thomas, USVI 00801
Email: pclyne14@gmail.com
Website: www.buildingblocksbvi.com
Telephone: (284) 495-9314
Facebook: www.facebook.com/peggy.clyne

AVAILABLE NOW

ISBN: 978-1-5127-0153-1 (sc)
ISBN: 978-1-5127-0154-8 (e)

More children's books:

My Mind is a Garden
My Body Is God's Temple

Printed in the United States
by Baker & Taylor Publisher Services